ALAN
SHEARER
A BIOGRAPHY

aydn Middleton

For Andrew and Calum, who know a good
player when they see one! H.M.

Acknowledgements
Photos: Action Images, pages 4, 8, 19. Rex Features, page 6. Empics Ltd / Don Morley, page
9. Rex Features / The Sun, page 10. Football Archive / Peter Robinson, pages 13, 18, 22, 23.
Empics Ltd, pages 15, 16, 21, 25, 26, 27. Laurence Griffiths / Empics Ltd, page 20. Empics
Ltd / Michael Steele, page 28. Allsport, page 29.

Heinemann Educational Publishers
Halley Court, Jordan Hill, Oxford OX2 8EJ
a division of Reed Educational & Professional Publishing Limited
www.heinemann.co.uk

Heinemann is a registered trademark of Reed Educational & Professional
Publishing Limited

First published 2000
Original edition © Haydn Middleton, 1999
Literacy Satellites edition © Haydn Middleton, 2000
Additional writing for Satellites edition by Christine Butterworth.

04
10 9 8 7 6 5 4 3

ISBN 0 435 11986 9 *Alan Shearer: A Biography* single copy
ISBN 0 435 11990 7 *Alan Shearer: A Biography* 6 copy pack

Designed by M2
Printed and bound in Scotland by Scotprint

Also available at Stage 4 Literacy World Satellites
ISBN 0 435 11988 5   *LW Satellites: Big Issues* single copy
ISBN 0 435 11992 3   *LW Satellites: Big Issues* 6 copy pack

ISBN 0 435 11989 3   *LW Satellites: Quakes, Floods and Other Disasters* single copy
ISBN 0 435 11993 1   *LW Satellites: Quakes, Floods and Other Disasters* 6 copy pack

ISBN 0 435 11987 7   *LW Satellites: Spiders (and how they hunt)* single copy
ISBN 0 435 11991 5   *LW Satellites: Spiders (and how they hunt)* 6 copy pack

ISBN 0 435 11995 8   *LW Satellites: Teachers' Guide Stage 4*
ISBN 0 435 11994 X   *LW Satellites: Guided Reading Cards Stage 4*

Contents

THERE'S ONLY ONE ALAN SHEARER

The England team won the World Cup in 1966, and they were kings of the football world until Brazil won it in June 1970. In August 1970 a baby boy was born in the north-east of England. Twenty-six years later that boy was captain of England. His name was Alan Shearer, and he wanted only one thing: to lead England to the World Cup crown again.

Top footballers earn lots of money, but Alan is very down-to-earth about it.
'We are very overpaid compared to doctors and nurses.'

The big man

Alan was England's best striker of the 1990s. Everything about him is big – from the number of goals he scores to the size of his transfer fees. His first transfer, in 1992, was from Southampton to Blackburn Rovers for £3.3 million. Kenny Dalglish, Blackburn's manager, said 'He's priceless. Shearer lifts the whole team.'

Alan was top scorer in the 1996 European Championships. That year he transferred from Blackburn to Newcastle United for £15 million. This was 22 times his own weight in gold!

Football has made Alan rich, but he still has a boy's love of the game.

'He gives 100% all the time,' says ex-footballer Glenn Roeder. Managers like that – and so do fans.

WORLD CUP WINNERS

1930	Uruguay	1970	Brazil
1934	Italy	1974	West Germany
1938	Italy	1978	Argentina
1950	Uruguay	1982	Italy
1954	West Germany	1986	Argentina
1958	Brazil	1990	Germany
1962	Brazil	1994	Brazil
1966	England	1998	France

Kevin Keegan was Alan's boyhood hero. Keegan thrilled Newcastle fans in the 1980s.

GEORDIE BOY

Alan was born in the Gosforth area of Newcastle on 13 August 1970. He's a 'Geordie', the nickname for people born in Newcastle. 'I played football every day as a lad,' he recalls, 'with a can if I couldn't find a proper ball.' His dad was a great Newcastle United fan.

Alan became a Newcastle supporter too, and a fan of Kevin Keegan. Kevin's skills helped Newcastle go up from the Second to the First Division, the top division in 1984. (There was no Premier League then.) Alan dreamed of being a Newcastle striker like Kevin. Years later his hero would help to make that dream come true.

He made up his mind to win

Alan played a lot of football at school. He played for two boys' clubs as well, scoring dozens of goals. He was a star of the county Under-19 team when he was only 15. As a player, Alan had three problems: he was small for his age, he couldn't run very fast, and he couldn't kick well with his left foot. But he had made up his mind to be a professional footballer. 'No one and nothing was going to stop him,' says his dad.

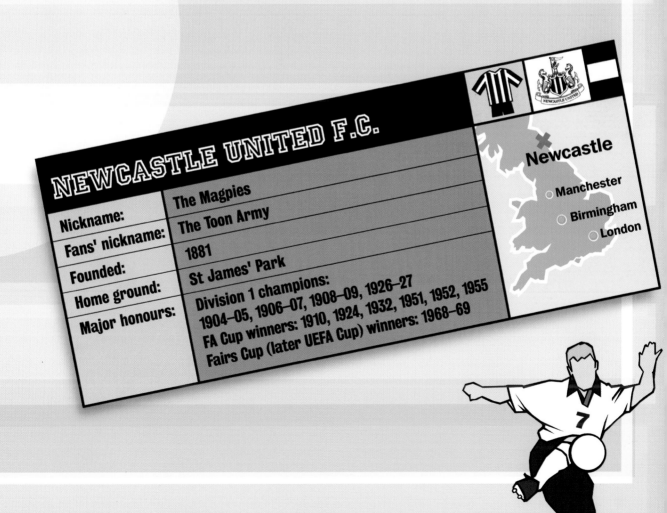

NEWCASTLE UNITED F.C.

Nickname:	The Magpies
Fans' nickname:	The Toon Army
Founded:	1881
Home ground:	St James' Park
Major honours:	Division 1 champions: 1904–05, 1906–07, 1908–09, 1926–27 1951, 1952, 1955 FA Cup winners: 1910, 1924, 1932, Fairs Cup (later UEFA Cup) winners: 1968–69

Newcastle

Manchester

Birmingham

London

Matthew Le Tissier – another young Saint
who would go on to great things

THE SAINT

Big professional clubs send 'scouts' all
over the country. They look for the stars of
the future in boys' teams. Several scouts
spotted Alan. Jack Hixon was a scout for Southampton. He
thought Alan could be a great striker. Jack says, 'He had the
essentials: attitude, application and character.'

Jack arranged a trial for Alan at his club, Southampton, and
the club signed him as a schoolboy in 1984. When he left
school, two years later, Southampton would have the first
chance to sign him as a trainee professional.

SOUTHAMPTON F.C.		
Nickname:	The Saints	
Founded:	1885	
Home ground:	The Dell	
Major honours:	Division 1 runners-up: 1983–84 FA Cup winners: 1976	

Manchester

Birmingham

London

Southampton

Going south

In 1984 'the Saints' were a top English club. In 1986 they signed Alan as a trainee, just before he was sixteen. He had to move 300 miles south, but Dave Merrington, the youth team coach said, 'Alan was never homesick.'

Alan was a youth team player for two seasons. He trained hard and got more skilful. He scored over 75 goals. His team mates called him Smokey because he was mad on Smokey Bacon crisps. Team-mate Matthew le Tissier had more natural talent, but 'Alan will always make the most of what he's got,' Jack Hixon had said, and Alan was in the first team before he was eighteen.

Peter Shilton, a Saint who won
125 caps for England

Alan married Lainya Arnold in 1991. Their first daughter, Chloe, was born in 1992.

HAT-TRICK HERO

Southampton had a bad season in 1987-8. Alan was scoring well for the youth team, so he was put in the first team. On 8 April 1988 he ran on to the field for the first time against mighty Arsenal. Within 49 minutes he had scored three goals.

His goals helped Southampton win 4-2. He was only 17 years and 240 days old – the youngest ever player to score a hat trick in the top division. The other players signed the ball and gave it to him – then told him it was his turn to wash the kit! But his kit-washing days were nearly over – he went professional four days later.

Shearer's League goal record at Southampton 1987–1992.

SEASON	APPEARANCES	GOALS
1987–88	8 appearances	3 goals
1988–89	10 appearances	0 goals
1989–90	26 appearances	3 goals
1990–91	36 appearances	4 goals
1991–92	41 appearances	13 goals

Goal trickle

In his first four seasons for Southampton, Alan scored only twenty goals, but he was highly valued in the team. Team-mate Jason Dodd said, 'You also need people to make the right runs off the ball and unsettle defences.' The fans valued him as an unselfish team player, and voted him 1991 Player of the Year. The England Under-21 team coaches valued him too...

THREE LIONS ON HIS SHIRT

As a boy, Alan's ambition was to play for England, '...the same as almost every boy in Newcastle,' he says. He made it in 1987 in the Under-17 side against the Republic of Ireland – and scored. In 1990 came his first game for the Under-21s, also against the Republic of Ireland. This time he scored twice. By 1991 he was captain, and led his country's team to a win at a tournament in France. He scored seven goals in four games.

This table shows how England has performed in European Championships and World Cups since Alan Shearer was born.

DATE	CHAMPIONSHIP	RESULT
1970	World Cup	Quarter finals
1972	European Championships	Quarter finals
1974	World Cup	Did not qualify
1976	European Championships	Did not qualify
1978	World Cup	Did not qualify
1980	European Championships	First round
1982	World Cup	Second round
1984	European Championships	Did not qualify
1986	World Cup	Quarter finals
1988	European Championships	First round
1990	World Cup	Semi finals
1992	European Championships	First round
1994	World Cup	Did not qualify
1996	European Championships	Semi finals
1998	World Cup	Second round

Getting better all the time

The full England team was getting ready for the 1992 European Championships. Alan was chosen to play in a friendly match at Wembley in February 1992. He scored the first goal in a 2-0 win against France. Alan won his cap, and played in the Euro '92 squad, but the team were knocked out without a win.

His Southampton manager, Ian Branfoot, still believed in Alan: 'He is a grafter.... you only have to tell him once and he does it. So if you think he's a good player now, just wait – he's going to be better.'

Alan in his first England game in 1992, against France

13

RECORD BREAKER

After six years at Southampton, Alan moved back to the north of England in 1992. His new club was Blackburn Rovers.

Jack Walker, Blackburn's rich chairman, and manager Kenny Dalglish, paid a record £3.3 million transfer fee. Alan was now England's top striker – and people wanted him to take Blackburn to the top of the new Premier League.

Southampton fans would miss Alan. The town's evening newspaper said, 'He has this city's best wishes going with him. Alan Shearer has always conducted himself well.'

BLACKBURN ROVERS F.C.

Nickname:	Rovers
Founded:	1875
Home ground:	Ewood Park
Major honours:	Premiership Champions: 1994–95 Division 1 champions: 1911–12, 1913–14 FA Cup winners: 1884, 1885, 1890, 1891, 1928

× Blackburn
○ Manchester
○ Birmingham
○ London

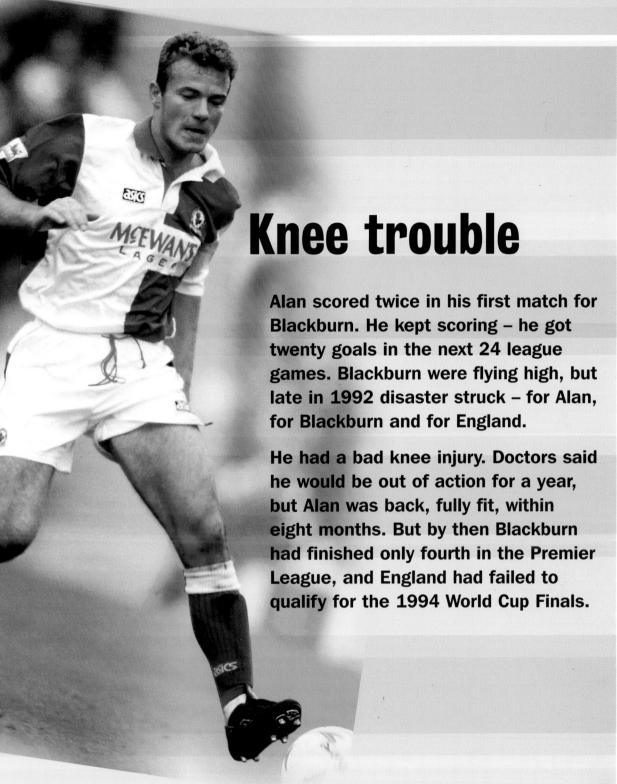

Knee trouble

Alan scored twice in his first match for Blackburn. He kept scoring – he got twenty goals in the next 24 league games. Blackburn were flying high, but late in 1992 disaster struck – for Alan, for Blackburn and for England.

He had a bad knee injury. Doctors said he would be out of action for a year, but Alan was back, fully fit, within eight months. But by then Blackburn had finished only fourth in the Premier League, and England had failed to qualify for the 1994 World Cup Finals.

Alan in action for Blackburn, 1992

15

CHAMPIONS!

Manchester United won the Premier League in 1992-3, for the first time since 1966-7. They won again the next season. Blackburn came second, helped by 31 League goals scored by Alan.

Blackburn now had several star players: Tim Flowers, David Batty and Chris Sutton. Strikers Shearer and Sutton were known as 'SAS', and they were a winning duo for Blackburn the following season.

The Premier League table at the end of Blackburn's championship season

TEAM	P	HOME			AWAY			POINTS
		W	D	L	W	D	L	
Blackburn Rovers	42	17	2	2	10	6	5	89
Manchester United	42	16	4	1	10	6	5	88
Nottingham Forest	42	12	6	3	10	5	6	77
Liverpool	42	13	5	3	8	6	7	74
Leeds	42	13	5	3	7	8	6	73
Newcastle	42	14	6	1	6	6	9	72
Tottenham Hotspur	42	10	5	6	6	9	6	62
Queens Park Rangers	42	11	3	7	6	6	9	60
Wimbledon	42	9	5	7	6	6	9	56
Southampton	42	8	9	4	4	9	8	54

Champions after 81 years

Shearer and Sutton kept Blackburn at the top of the table for most of the 1994-5 championship. Manchester United were close behind, but Blackburn beat them by one point in the last game of the season. Blackburn were champions for the first time since 1914.

It was Alan's perfect season – he had a championship medal and he was the Premier League's top goalscorer. To add to this, Blackburn fans and the Professional Footballers' Association both voted him Player of the Year.

SHORT OF GOALS

Football is a team game. Alan was a great striker – but he depended on his Blackburn team-mates to supply the passes that he could hammer into the net. He kept scoring during the 1995-96 season: 31 goals, including five hat-tricks.

Blackburn's defenders let them down, however. They finished only seventh in the League. Alan had kept scoring for Blackburn, but it was a different story when he played for England.

Alan's place in peril?

The 1996 European Championship Finals were to be played in England, so the England team did not have to qualify. During the 21 months run-up, they played many friendly games to warm up. Amazingly, in 12 games Alan did not score a goal. Newspapers began saying his Euro '96 place should go to Newcastle's Les Ferdinand or Liverpool's Robbie Fowler.

But Alan and the England manager, Terry Venables, still believed he was England's best striker. Venables picked Alan for the first match of Euro '96, against Switzerland.

Alan's family supports him in good times and bad.

19

GOLDEN BOOT

Alan gave his critics something to think about. He stormed back with the first goal in a 1-1 draw against Switzerland. A Shearer header helped England to a 2-0 win against Scotland. He capped this by scoring twice in a storming 4-1 win against Holland. Then England met Spain in the quarter-finals.

That match was a goalless draw, and had to be decided on penalties. Alan took the first England kick – and put England on the path to victory. Now mighty Germany waited, in the semi-final.

So near – yet so far

Alan put England 1-0 up three minutes into the game. But Germany soon drew level, and the game went to a draw, which meant another penalty shoot-out. Alan scored the first, but Gareth Southgate missed the sixth, and England were out. Germany went on to win Euro '96.

Defeat was painful, but Alan had shown he could score goals at the highest international level. He won the 'Golden Boot' for being the top scorer in Euro '96. Author Shaun Campbell wrote in his 1997 biography (life story) of Alan, 'The world was now at his feet, but only a few clubs would be able to afford him.'

Alan with Euro '96 team-mates Paul Gascoigne and Teddy Sheringham

BACK HOME

'Yes, we've got the big one we wanted. This is for the people of Newcastle.'

These are the words of Kevin Keegan, ex-England captain and former Newcastle United star. Now Newcastle manager, he had just signed up Alan Shearer. It was July 1996. Newcastle had to pay Blackburn a world record fee of £15 million.

Alan at his first Newcastle press conference, between chairman Sir John Hall and manager Kevin Keegan

22

When Alan joined Newcastle, the club shop sold £70,000 worth of number nine shirts.

Return of the hero

Crowds of Newcastle fans came to the ground when they heard of Alan's transfer. There had been reports that he would sign abroad, or for Manchester United, but in the end he had come home. If he could score as well for Newcastle as he had at Blackburn, the Magpies could take on the Champions, Manchester United.

Alan said that Keegan was part of the reason he came home: 'I wanted to play for Newcastle. He didn't have to sell it to me. I was talking to one of my heroes, a man I had paid to watch as a kid.'

RUNNERS UP

The 1996-97 Newcastle team held a lot of talent. Besides Alan there were David Ginola, Faustino Asprilla, Peter Beardsley and Les Ferdinand, Alan's new strike partner.

Despite more injury problems, Alan kept scoring goals. He was top Premiership scorer, with 25 goals in 31 League games. Leicester City fans saw Alan's goal-scoring skill. Their team was winning 3-1. Then Alan scored a hat-trick to give Newcastle a 4-3 win. He was PFA Player of the Year again at the season's end, but this time there was no championship medal to go with the award.

TEAM		HOME			AWAY			POINTS
	P	W	D	L	W	D	L	
Manchester United	38	12	5	2	9	7	3	75
Newcastle United	38	13	3	3	6	8	5	68
Arsenal	38	10	5	4	9	6	4	68
Liverpool	38	10	6	3	9	5	5	68
Aston Villa	38	11	5	3	6	5	8	61
Chelsea	38	9	8	2	7	3	9	59
Sheffield Wednesday	38	8	10	1	6	5	8	57
Wimbledon	38	9	6	4	6	5	8	56
Leicester City	38	7	5	7	5	6	8	47
Tottenham Hotspur	38	8	4	7	5	3	11	46

The Premier League table at the end of the 1996–97 season. Manchester United were top of the table, but Newcastle beat them 5–0 in one famous match.

Back with King Kenny

Newcastle finished the season as runners-up to Manchester United. Kevin Keegan had quit because of the huge pressure he felt to succeed. In his place was another football idol – Kenny Dalglish, Alan's old manager at Blackburn.

Kevin said later, 'My proudest achievement was that I brought Alan Shearer home...we got the greatest of all.' Kenny just said, 'I'm lost for words when it comes to describing Shearer's achievements.'

In 1996–97 Alan failed to score against only three teams: Middlesborough, West Ham and his old club, Southampton.

25

Alan loves his country. 'Not many things beat skippering your country,' he says. 'It's a great honour.'

CAPTAIN MARVEL

On 1 September 1996 England kicked off against Moldova in their first qualifying game of the 1998 World Cup. Alan was team skipper. 'Alan's a special player, and I hope being captain gives him even greater power,' said the new England manager, Glenn Hoddle.

Alan scored in the first game and England won 3-0, and scored four more times in the next four games. England ended the season beating France in a friendly match. Things looked good for the 1997-98 lead-up to the World Cup finals.

Alan was unlucky when Newcastle lost to Arsenal in the 1998 Cup Final.

Struck down again

Injury hit Alan in a pre-season friendly match and stopped him from playing for months. Newcastle ended up only thirteenth in the Premiership, though England still qualified for the World Cup finals.

But all was not quite lost. Alan came back before the end of the season, scoring five goals to help Newcastle into their first FA Cup Final since 1974. Then bad luck struck again and Alan's shot hit the post. Arsenal went on to win the Cup 2-0.

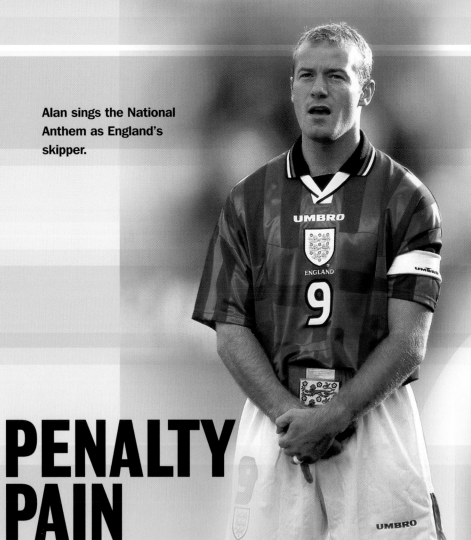

Alan sings the National Anthem as England's skipper.

PENALTY PAIN

Alan was England's skipper again for their first group match against Tunisia in the World Cup in June 1998. He and the fans shared the same dream – that England might win the World Cup for the first time since 1966.

Alan scored first from a pass by Graham Le Saux. A late goal from Paul Scholes made sure of a 2-0 win for England. Their joy did not last long – they lost 1-2 to Romania. They would have to beat Colombia to go through to the second stage.

New star striker

Alan had a new strike partner against the Colombians. Fans called Liverpool's 18-year-old Michael Owen 'the next Alan Shearer'. The pair helped England to a 2-0 win. Now England had to face Argentina.

This was a huge match for Alan. Owen and Shearer scored; then Argentina got two goals back before half-time. At the end of extra time, the score was still 2-2. Just as in Euro '96, there had to be a penalty shoot-out. Alan scored, but Paul Ince and David Batty missed, and England were out of the competition. Alan's dream was over for another four years.

THE FIRST ELEVEN SEASONS

Alan first played in the top division in 1987-88. These tables show all his club games and the goals he scored. In the same period he was capped 43 times, and scored 20 goals for England.

For Southampton FC

Year	Competition	Appearances	Goals
1987–88	League	3 (plus 2 as a sub)	3
1988–89	League	8 (2)	0
1989–90	League	19 (7)	3
	FA Cup	1 (0)	0
	Littlewoods Cup	4 (2)	2
	Total	**24 (9)**	**5**
1990–91	League	34 (2)	4
	FA Cup	3 (1)	2
	Rumbelows Cup	6 (0)	6
	ZDS Cup	2 (0)	2
	Total	**45 (3)**	**14**
1991–92	League	41 (0)	13
	FA Cup	7 (0)	2
	Rumbelows Cup	6 (0)	3
	ZDS Cup	6 (0)	3
	Total	**60 (0)**	**21**

For Blackburn Rovers FC

Year	Competition	Appearances	Goals
1992–93	League	21 (0)	16
	Coca-Cola Cup	5 (0)	6
	Total	**26 (0)**	**22**
1993–94	League	34 (6)	31
	FA Cup	4 (0)	2
	Coca-Cola Cup	4 (0)	1
	Total	**42 (6)**	**34**
1994–95	League	42 (0)	34
	FA Cup	2 (0)	0
	Coca-Cola Cup	3 (0)	2
	UEFA Cup	2 (0)	1
	Total	**49 (0)**	**37**
1995–96	League	35 (0)	31
	FA Cup	2 (0)	0
	Coca-Cola Cup	4 (0)	5
	European Cup	6 (0)	1
	Charity Shield	1 (0)	0
	Total	**48 (0)**	**37**

For Newcastle United FC

Year	Competition	Appearances	Goals
1996–97	League	31 (0)	25
	FA Cup	3 (0)	1
	Coca-Cola Cup	1 (0)	1
	UEFA Cup	4 (0)	1
	Charity Shield	1 (0)	0
	Total	**40 (0)**	**28**
1997–98	League	15 (2)	2
	FA Cup	6 (0)	5
	Total	**21 (2)**	**7**

Index